YO-DJQ-384

THE BIG FEARON EARLY LEARNING BOOK

CHARLES BENNETT
1271 GROVELAND LANE
LAKELAND, FL 33811

THE BIG FEARON EARLY LEARNING BOOK

by Jean Marzollo and illustrated by Beth Savage

Fearon Teacher Aids • A division of **PITMAN LEARNING, INC.**
Belmont, California

 **MAKEMASTER®**
Blackline Masters

Editorial director: Roberta Suid
Production editor: Mary McClellan
Production services: The Bookmakers, Inc.
Designer: Beth Savage, Stan Tusan
Illustrator: Beth Savage
Cover designer: Bill Nagel

Entire contents copyright © 1981 by Jean Marzollo and Beth Savage. Permission is hereby granted
to reproduce materials in this book for noncommercial classroom use. All other uses
require permission from Pitman Learning, Inc., 6 Davis Drive,
Belmont, California 94002. Member of the Pitman Group.

ISBN-0-8224-4476-3
Printed in the United States of America.

1. 9 8 7 6 5 4

Contents

Foreword

The *Big Fearon Early Learning Book* provides the teacher with duplicatable pages that focus on the basic skills involved in using numbers and letters, in storytelling, and in thinking. The four parts of the book correspond to standard units in the preschool and primary curricula.

Each part of the book opens with a letter that can be sent home to parents when the unit is first introduced to students. In this way, the parents are informed of the work the child is doing in school. As the child brings the worksheets home, the parents will be able to follow the child's progress and discuss the work with the child. These letters help to promote parental involvement in the student's school activities.

Each unit also contains directions to the teacher. These directions provide an explanation of the purpose of the worksheets and an instructional model for their use. You'll also find information about the basic skills that are developed as the students complete the worksheets. The teacher should always feel free to adapt the worksheets in a way that best suits his or her instructional objectives.

The 176 blackline masters are the heart of the units. Students will learn as they practice such skills as cutting, counting, telling stories out loud, matching, classifying, and writing. Each page is designed to keep the student busily active and motivated. The appealing illustrations, many of which are designed to be cut out or colored, are an extra bonus.

The Editors

NUMBERS AND NUMBER VALUES

Dear Parents,

This year your child will be bringing home mathematics worksheets to show you. Sometimes the worksheets will be homework. In these cases, your child is to do the work and bring it back to school the next day. Sometimes your child will have completed the worksheet in school and will be bringing it home to show you what he or she has done.

Your child will learn various mathematics skills during the year. First, the child will learn to recognize numerals. (We call written numbers "numerals.") When you point out the numeral 3, your child will be able to say, "Three."

Second, the child will learn to write numerals. Your child will be proud to show you his or her writing skills.

Third, your child will learn that each numeral stands for a certain value and will be able to show an understanding of that value. If you write the numeral 5 on a piece of paper and say, "Bring me this many spoons," your child will be able to do it.

Finally, your child will learn to sequence numerically. This means that the child will be able to put things in order according to amount.

At home you can help your child learn about the world of mathematics by talking about the numerals on the bathroom scale, on the outdoor thermometer, on measuring cups, on the clock, on the radio dial, on the telephone, and on rulers. In this way you will be helping your child realize that numbers are a part of everyday life.

Thank you,

Your child's teacher

Directions for Teachers

The purpose of this part is to teach children to recognize numerals, to write numerals, to learn the value of numerals, and to learn to sequence numerically. The part should also give children an understanding of the use of numbers in the world around them. All of the pages in this part can be colored by the children. Certain related pages may be saved and stapled together. For specific page directions, see below.

Pages 5-6

Ask the children to use light-colored crayons so that the numerals will show through after the objects have been colored. They may color the entire object that has a numeral on it (such as the whole scale), or they may prefer to color only the part of the object that has numerals on it (such as the circle on the scale). Ask the children to look around the classroom to find real objects with numerals on them.

Pages 7-8

Use these two pages for assessing whether or not the children can recognize numerals. Before you begin, make sure the children know their colors. Have crayons available.

Pages 9-10

In these visual discrimination exercises, the children discriminate numerals from other written marks. Suggest that the children point to each written mark and say to themselves silently, "Is this a numeral? If so, I will circle it. If not, I will leave it alone."

Pages 11-20

Demonstrate at the chalkboard how to write each numeral. Whenever you teach a new numeral, hand out the appropriate worksheet. Show the children how to write each numeral, following the arrows in the correct sequence. Ask the children to count and color the objects. Pages 11-20 can be saved and stapled together to make a large counting book.

Pages 21-22

These two pages can be pasted together, cut, and assembled to make a small counting book. Give the children copies of pages 21 and 22. Ask them to count the objects, write in the numerals, and color the pictures. Then show them how to paste the blank sides of the worksheets together. Let the pages dry overnight. The next day, show the children how to cut the pages on the dotted lines. Warn them not to cut down the middle on the solid lines. Stack the cut pages like this:

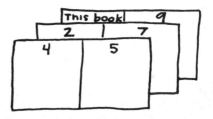

Then fold them in the middle to make a small book. The pages can be stapled together on the fold line.

Pages 23-25

These pages deal with the value of the numerals 1-8. Tell the children to count one row of pictures at a time. Show the children how to draw a line from that row to the correct numeral. The line doesn't have to be straight. It can curve around like a road.

Pages 26-28

These pages deal with the value of the numerals 1-10. Tell the children to count the objects, circle the correct numeral underneath, and color the pictures.

Pages 29-32

Before using these pages, introduce the numeral and concept "zero." On the worksheets, the children draw the number of objects indicated in the pictures. Tell the children they can make their pictures any way they like, as long as they draw the correct number of objects and put them in the right places.

Pages 33-35

On these worksheets, the children count objects and write the correct numeral in the box. Page 33 works with the numerals 1-5, page 34 with the numerals 4-8, and page 35 with the numerals 5-10.

4

Pages 36–37

Again, the children count objects and write the correct numeral in the box. Page 37 may stimulate a discussion about how eggs are packed by the dozen and half dozen. You might want to collect egg cartons for use in counting games.

Pages 38–39

These follow-the-dot pages are useful for assessing whether or not children know the correct sequence of numbers from 1 to 10.

Page 40

The number squares on this worksheet are one inch square. When the children paste these squares in the correct order, they will have a paper ruler to cut out and use for measuring.

Pages 41–42

Suggest that the children first guess the missing number, then count the objects below to check their guesses.

Pages 43–45

Tell the children to count the objects on the worksheets and write down the correct numeral on each picture. On page 43, they can write the numeral on one of the balloons. On pages 44 and 45, they can write beside or below the bananas and grapes. After writing the numerals, the children cut out the pictures and put them in order from 1 to 10.

Pages 46–48

On these last three pages, the children work with graphs. Show them how to figure out where each picture goes on page 46. Which thing is in just one picture? That picture goes next to the numeral 1. Which thing is in two pictures? Those pictures go next to the 2, and so forth. For page 48, help the children take a poll about pets and make graphs of the results. They might also make graphs showing the results of polls about cars, sports teams, TV stars, and so on.

name _____

Color each thing that has numerals on it.

by J. Marzollo and B. Savage

Numbers & Number Values copyright ©1981

Learning to recognize numerals.

name _____

Color each thing that has numerals on it.

Learning to recognize numerals.

Numbers & Number Values copyright © 1981 by J. Marzollo and R. Savage

name _____

Color the numeral 1 red.
Color the numeral 2 green.
Color the numeral 3 blue.
Color the numeral 4 yellow.
Color the numeral 5 orange.

by J. Marzollo and B. Savage

Numbers & Number Values copyright© 1981

Learning to recognize numerals.

name _____

Color the numeral 6 red.
Color the numeral 7 green.
Color the numeral 8 blue.
Color the numeral 9 yellow.
Color the numeral 10 orange.

Learning to recognize numerals.

name _____

Circle the numerals, not the letters.

A

2

D

10

M

C

B

20

3

R

X

9

4

2

L

H

6

F

7

8

5

P

E

S

N

by J. Marzollo and B. Savage

Numbers & Number Values copyright©1981

Learning to recognize numerals.

name _____

Circle the numerals, not the squiggles.

8

3

7

2

(squiggles)

1   6

5

9

4

10

14

Learning to recognize numerals.

Numbers & Number Values copyright © 1991 by J. Marzollo and B. Sawyer

name _____

Write the numerals. Count and color the pictures.

by J. Marzollo and B. Savage

Numbers & Number Values copyright©1981

Learning to write numerals.

12

name _____

Write the numerals. Count and color the pictures.

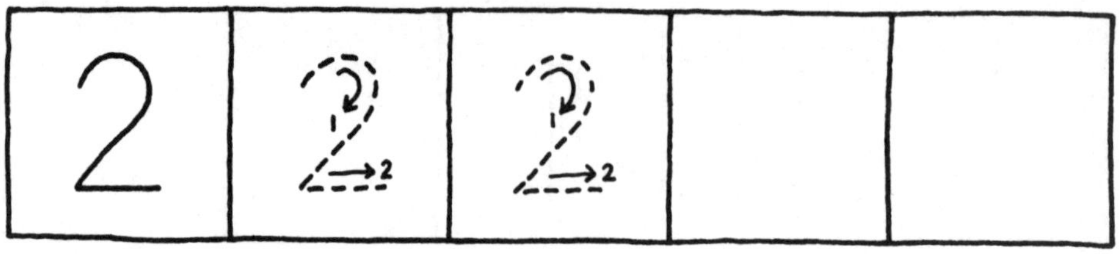

| 2 | 2 | 2 | | |

name _____

Write the numerals. Count and color the pictures.

by J. Marzollo and B. Savage

Numbers & Number Values copyright©1981

Learning to write numerals.

name _____

Write the numerals. Count and color the pictures.

4	4	4		

Learning to write numerals.

Numbers & Number Values copyright © 1981 by L Mezzelle and B Savage

name _____

Write the numerals. Count and color the pictures.

| 5 | 5 | 5 | | |

Learning to write numerals.

by J. Marzollo and B. Savage

Numbers & Number Values copyright©1981

name _____

Write the numerals. Count and color the pictures.

| 6 | 6 | 6 | | |

name _____

Write the numerals. Count and color the pictures.

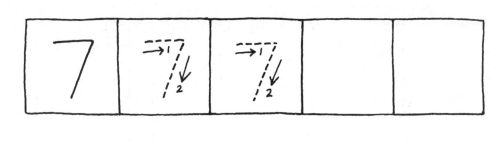

Learning to write numerals.

name _____

Write the numerals. Count and color the pictures.

8	8	8		

Numbers & Number Values copyright © 1981   by J. Marzollo and B. Savage

name _____

Write the numerals. Count and color the pictures.

| 9 | 9 | 9 | | |

Learning to write numerals.

name _____

Write the numerals. Count and color the pictures.

Learning to write numerals.

Make your own counting book.
Cut on dotted lines. Assemble and fold on solid lines.

by J. Marzollo and D. Savage copyright © 1981

Numbers & Number Values

10

My Very Own Counting Book

8

1

6

3

22

This book
belongs to

_____

9

2

7

4

5

name _____

Count. Draw a line to the correct numeral.

2

1

4

5

3

Learning the value of numerals.

name _____

Count. Draw a line to the correct numeral.

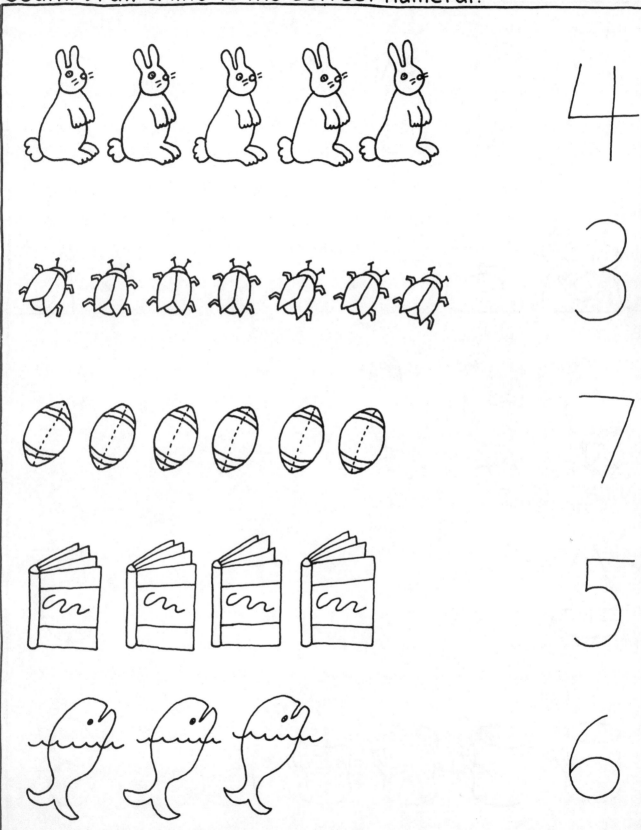

Numbers & Number Values copyright © 1991

Learning the value of numerals.

name _____

Count. Draw a line to the correct numeral.

6

8

4

7

5

Learning the value of numerals.

name _____

Count. Circle the correct numeral.

1 2 3 4 5

2 3 4 5 6

4 5 6 7 8

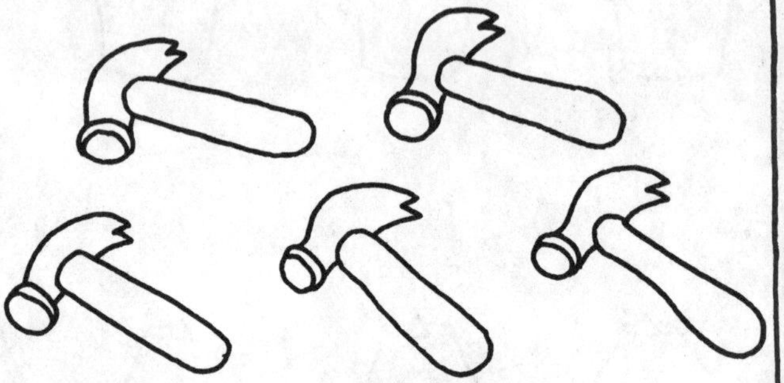

5 6 7 8 9

1 2 3 4 5

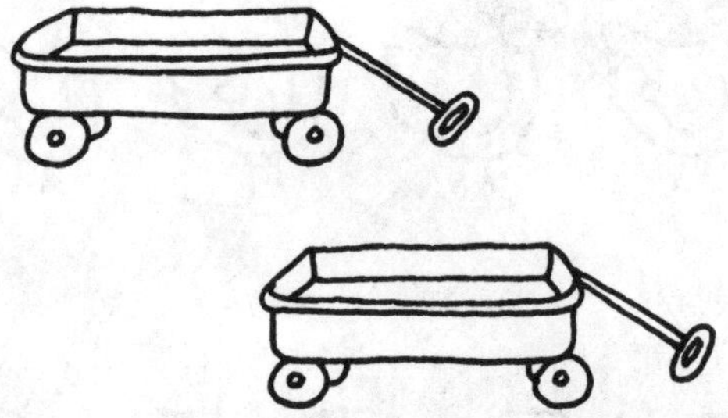

2 3 4 5 6

Learning the value of numerals.

name _____

Count. Circle the correct numeral.

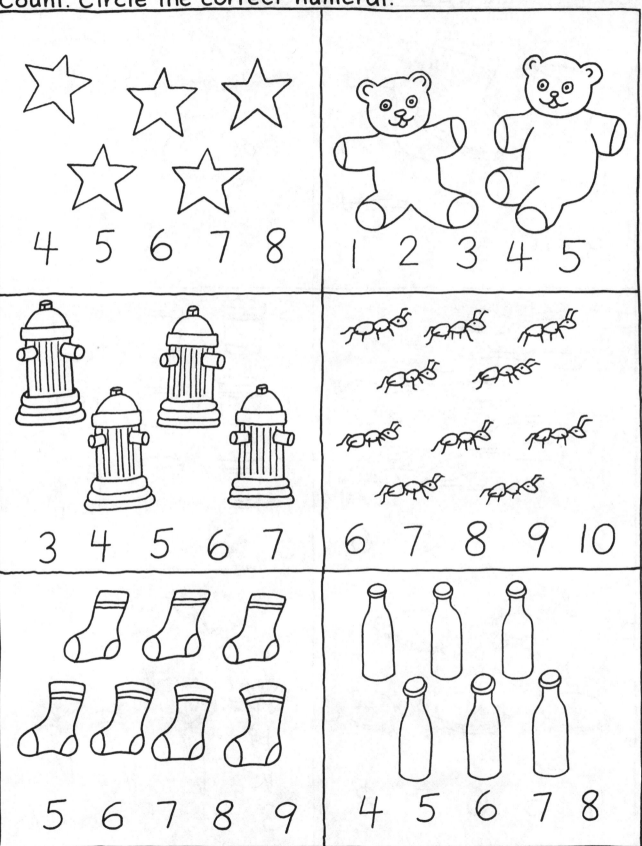

4   5   6   7   8

1   2   3   4   5

3   4   5   6   7

6   7   8   9   10

5   6   7   8   9

4   5   6   7   8

by J. Marzollo and B. Savage

Numbers & Number Values copyright © 1981

Learning the value of numerals.

name _____

Count. Circle the correct numeral.

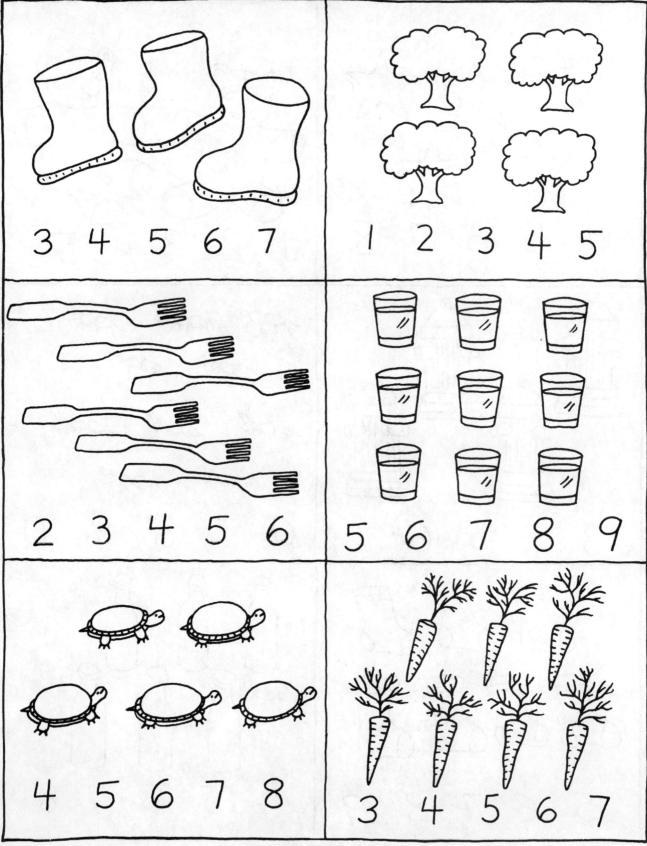

3 4 5 6 7

1 2 3 4 5

2 3 4 5 6

5 6 7 8 9

4 5 6 7 8

3 4 5 6 7

Learning the value of numerals.

name _____

Draw the right number of flowers in each vase.

by J. Marzollo and B. Savage

Numbers & Number Values copyright©1981

Learning the value of numerals.

name _____

Draw the right number of windows in each house.

3

0

1

5

4

Learning the value of numerals.

name _____

Fill in the numbers that are missing in each line.

Row 1: 1, 2, __, 4, 5, 6
Row 2: __, 2, 3, 4, __, 6
Row 3: 1, 2, 3, __, __, 6
Row 4: 1, __, __, 4, 5, 6
Row 5: 1, 2, __, __, __, 6

Learning to sequence numerically.

Numbers & Number Values copyright©1981 by J. Marzollo and R. Sovier

name _____

Draw the right number of people in each boat.

3

5

Learning the value of numerals.

by J. Marzollo and B. Savage

Numbers & Number Values copyright © 1981

32

name _____

Draw the right number of animals in the circus train.

Learning the value of numerals.

name _____

Count. Write the numeral in the box.

Learning the value of numerals.

name _____

Count. Write the numeral in the box.

by J. Marzollo and B. Savage

Numbers & Number Values copyright © 1981

Learning the value of numerals.

name _____

Count. Write the numeral in the box.

Learning the value of numerals.

name _____

Count. Write the numeral in the box.

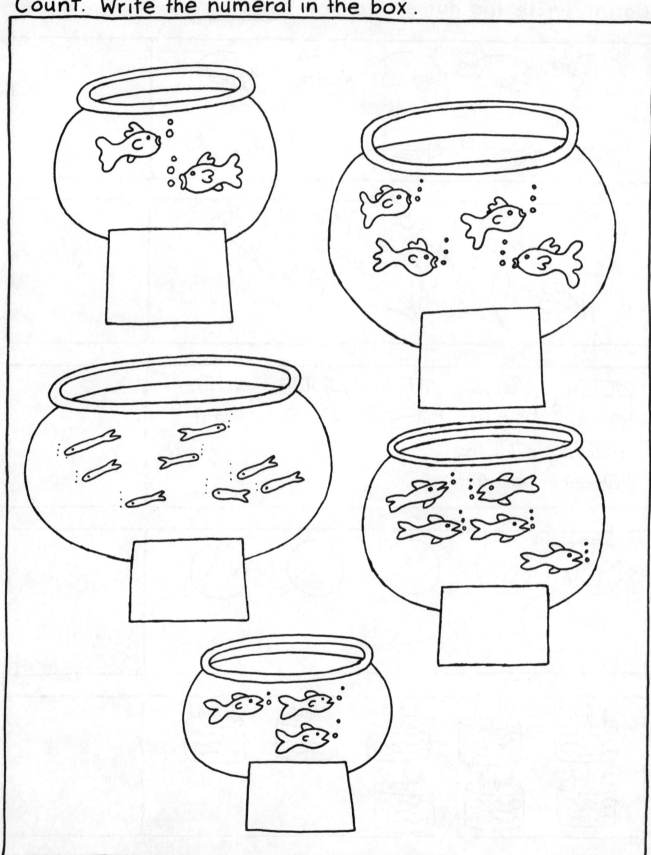

Numbers & Number Values copyright © 1981 by J. Marzollo and R. Savage

Learning the value of numerals.

name _____

Count. Write the numeral in the box.

By J. Marzollo and D. Savage   Numbers & Number Values copyright © 1981

Learning the value of numerals.

name _____

Follow the numerals from 1 to 10.

.7   .6

8.

.4

5.

.10

9.   3.

1.   .2

by J. Marzollo and B. Savage

Numbers & Number Values copyright © 1981

Learning to sequence numerically.

name _____

Follow the numerals from one to ten.

9

8

.5   .4

3   .2

7. .6

10   i

by J. Marzollo and B. Savage

Numbers & Number Values copyright © 1981

Learning to sequence numerically.

name _____

Cut out the numerals and paste them in order on the ruler.

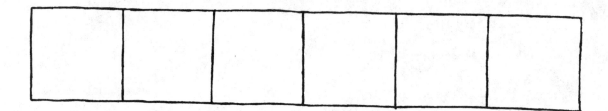

by J. Marzollo and B. Savage   copyright © 1981

Numbers & Number Values

Learning to sequence numerically.

name _____

Fill in the number that is missing in each line.

1 •	2 ••	3 •••	4 ••••
•	2 ••	3 •••	4 ••••
1 •	••	3 •••	4 ••••
1 •	2 ••	3 •••	••••

by J. Marzollo and B. Savage

Numbers & Number Values copyright© 1981

Learning to sequence numerically.

name _____

Cut out the clowns and put them in order from 1 to 6.

by J. Mazzola and D. Savage

Numbers & Number Values copyright © 1981

Learning to sequence numerically.

name _____

Cut out the bananas and put them in order from 1 to 10.

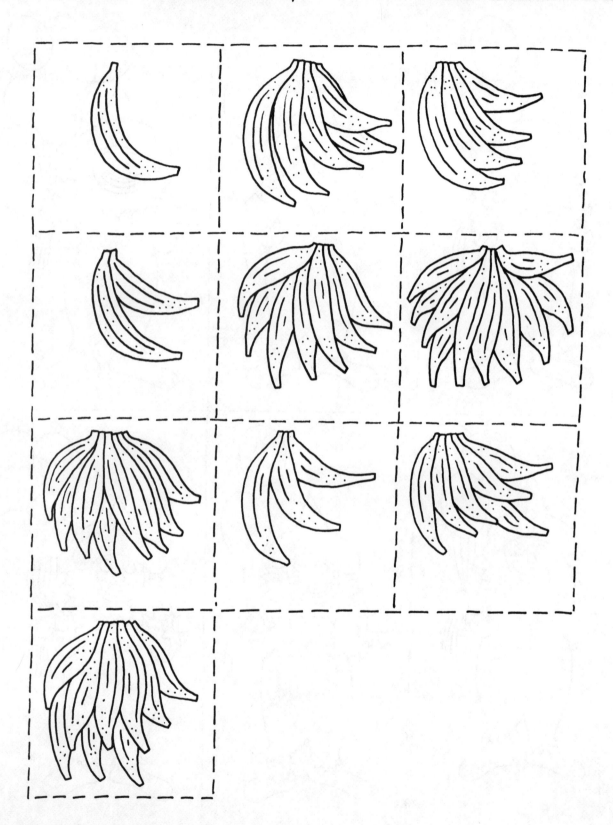

by J. Marzollo and R. Savage

Numbers & Number Values copyright© 1981

Learning to sequence numerically.

name _____

Cut out the grapes and put them in order from 1 to 10.

Learning to sequence numerically.

name _____

Cut out each animal and paste it where it fits on the graph.
Which animals do you have most of? Least of?

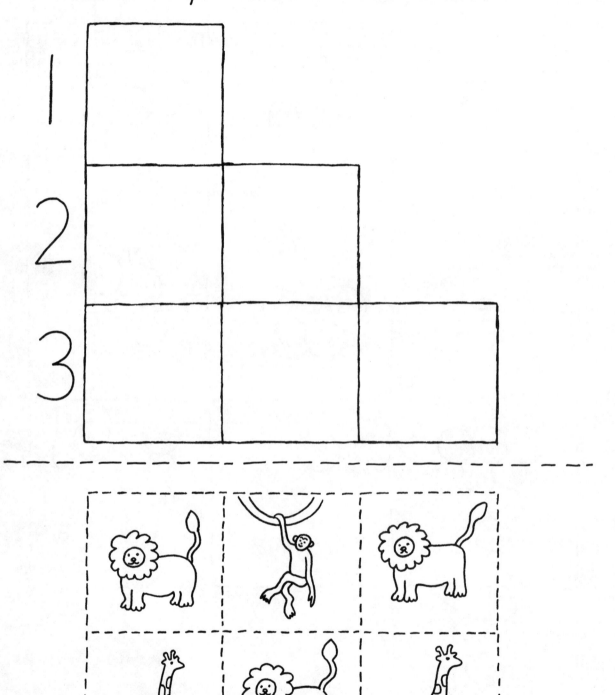

by J. Marzollo and B. Savage

Numbers & Number Values copyright © 1981

Learning to sequence numerically.

name _____

Cut out each hat and paste it where it fits on the graph.
Which hats do you have most of? Least of?

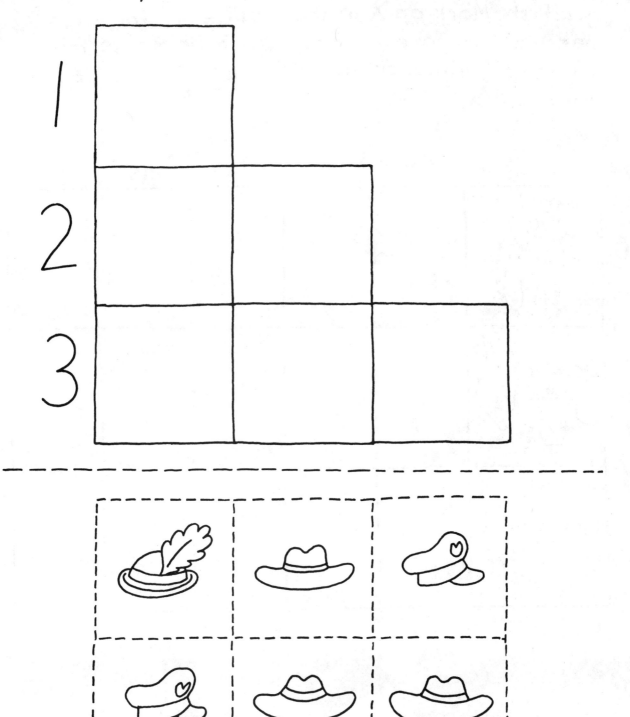

by J. Marzollo and D. Savage

Numbers & Number Values copyright © 1981

Learning to sequence numerically.

name _____

Favorite Pet Poll

Ask 5 people which they like best : cats, dogs, or goldfish. Mark an X in the right spot for each person. Compare results. Which animal is the favorite? Which animal is the least favorite?

by J. Marzollo and B. Savage

Numbers & Number Values copyright © 1981

Learning to sequence numerically.

LETTER SOUNDS

Dear Parents,

This year your child will be bringing home worksheets about letters and about the sounds that are associated with letters. Sometimes the worksheets will be homework. In these cases, your child is to do the work and bring it back to school the next day. Sometimes your child will have completed the worksheet in school and will be bringing it home to show you what he or she has done.

Understanding that letters are symbols for sounds is fundamental to the process of learning to read. These worksheets will help your child gain that understanding. You can help by going over the worksheets with your child. It will not be necessary for you to teach any skills beyond those that are found on each worksheet.

The most effective way you can help your child to become a good reader is to read out loud to him or her. Borrow books together from the library. Children who learn to love books early in life usually turn out to be good readers.

If you have any questions about prereading and reading skills, please feel free to get in touch with me.

Thank you,

Your child's teacher

Directions for Teachers

The purpose of this part is to teach children to discriminate initial sounds, associate sounds with letters, recognize words that rhyme, match initial sounds with letters, complete simple word families, and read simple word families.

All of the pages can be colored. The pictures on pages 55–88 can also be cut out and pasted into alphabet books that the children make. For specific directions, see below.

Pages 55–88

These pages give the children a chance to learn one letter sound at a time. First they practice consonants, then short vowels, then long vowels, and finally a few familiar blends.

We recommend that you use these pages to make alphabet or letter sounds books. Present each worksheet and letter sound in four steps, then compile the books in a fifth step as described below.

1. Discuss the letter sounds. Draw the letter for the day on the chalkboard and tell the children what sound it stands for. Ask the children to think of words that start with that sound. Look for objects in the classroom whose names start with that sound.

2. Color the worksheets. Hand out the worksheets. Direct the children to color only those pictures whose names begin with the sound for the day, and not the other pictures. Remind them that they will be saving the pictures that they color to put in a book. Point out that the picture in the upper right corner of the worksheet is the item mentioned in the directions.

Because some children may not recognize all the objects on the page, you may want to discuss each picture before the children begin to color. In this way, you can be certain that the children know the correct name of each object.

As the children finish, have them bring their worksheets to you for checking. Go over mistakes with each child individually. If the child has colored a picture whose name begins with the wrong sound, explain the error and ask the child to cross out that picture. If the child has missed a picture that should have been colored, explain the error and ask the child to correct it.

3. Cut and paste. Explain to the children that they

will each make a letter sounds book. Each worksheet that they have colored will provide pictures for one page of the book. The children should have colored construction paper for the pages of their letter sounds books.

After the children have completed a worksheet, tell them to cut out the pictures that they colored and paste these on one sheet of the construction paper. As the children finish, have them bring each new letter sound page to you.

4. Review. Use the letter sound page to review the letter and sound for the day with each child. If the child can write the letter, tell him or her to write both the capital and small form on the letter sound page. If some children cannot do this, write the letters on the pages for them.

Ask the child to think of an object whose name begins with the same sound as the things on the page. Tell the child to draw a picture of this object on the letter sound page.

After this review, put each child's work in an individual folder to save for the letter sounds books.

5. Compile the books. When the children have completed worksheets 55–88, return the letter sound pages you have saved in their individual folders. Help the children make construction paper covers for their books. Staple together the pages and the cover to make a book for each child to take home.

Pages 89–91

On these pages the children draw lines to connect words that rhyme. Show the children how the final letters of the rhyming words on these pages are the same. You may also ask the children to color each rhyming pair of pictures the same color. When the children have completed the task, have them "read" the rhyming pictures to you.

Pages 92–98

These pages further develop the concept of word families: words that rhyme and have endings that are spelled the same way. Go over page 92 out loud with the children, so they will see that by changing the first letter (and sound) of the words, they can change the meaning. After the children have finished their pages, ask them to read the words out loud to you.

name _____

Color the pictures that begin with the sound /b/ as in ball.

Listening to initial sounds.
Associating sounds with letters.

name _____

Color the pictures that begin with the sound /c/ as in cat.

name _____

Color the pictures that begin with the sound /d/ as in duck.

by J. Marzollo and B. Savage   Letter Sounds copyright © 1981

Listening to initial sounds.
Associating sounds with letters.

name _____

Color the pictures that begin with the sound /f/ as in fish.

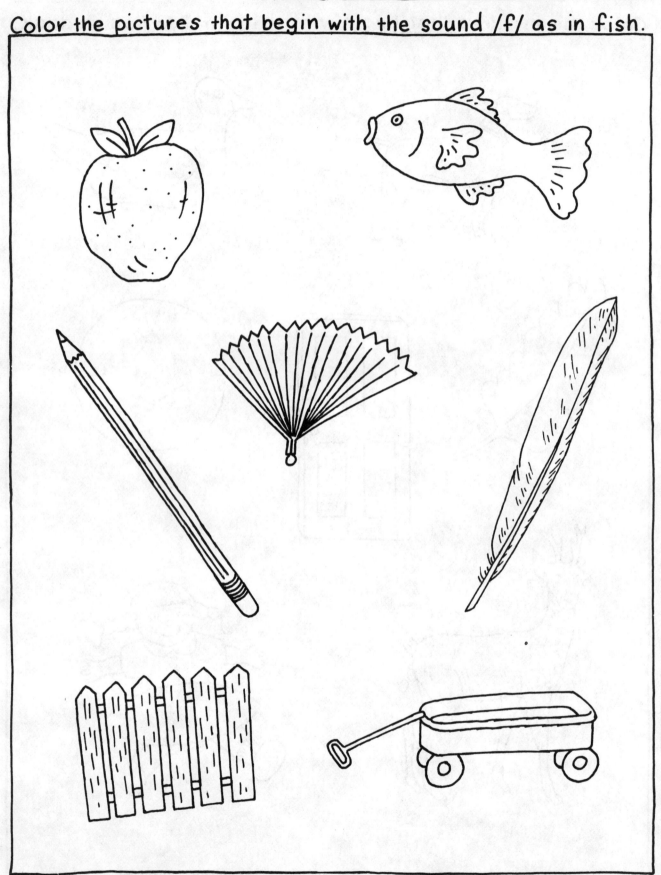

Listening to initial sounds.
Associating sounds with letters.

name _____

Color the pictures that begin with the sound /g/ as in goat.

Letter Sounds copyright© 1981 by J. Marzollo and D. Savage

Listening to initial sounds.
Associating sounds with letters.

name _____

Color the pictures that begin with the sound /h/ as in hat.

Letter Sounds copyright©1981   by J. Marzollo and B. Savage

Listening to initial sounds.
Associating sounds with letters.

name _____

Color the pictures that begin with the sound /j/ as in jar.

JELLY

by J. Marzollo and B. Savage

Letter Sounds copyright © 1981

Listening to initial sounds.
Associating sounds with letters.

name _____

Color the pictures that begin with the sound /k/ as in kite.

Listening to initial sounds.
Associating sounds with letters.

name _____

Color the pictures that begin with the sound /l/ as in lamp.

by J. Marzollo and B. Savage

Letter Sounds copyright© 1981

Listening to initial sounds.
Associating sounds with letters.

64

name _____

Color the pictures that begin with the sound /m/ as in mask.

Letter Sounds copyright© 1981   by J. Marzollo and B. Savage

Listening to initial sounds.
Associating sounds with letters.

name _____

Color the pictures that begin with the sound /n/ as in net.

by J. Marzollo and B. Savage

Letter Sounds copyright © 1981

Listening to initial sounds.
Associating sounds with letters.

name _____

Color the pictures that begin with the sound /p/ as in pig.

Letter Sounds copyright © 1981 by J. Marzollo and B. Savage

Listening to initial sounds.
Associating sounds with letters.

name _____

Color the pictures that begin with the sound /q/ as in queen.

by J. Marzollo and B. Savage

Letter Sounds copyright © 1981

Listening to initial sounds.
Associating sounds with letters.

68

name _____

Color the pictures that begin with the sound /r/ as in raccoon.

Listening to initial sounds.
Associating sounds with letters.

name _____

Color the pictures that begin with the sound /s/ as in sun.

by J. Marzollo and B. Savage

Letters Sounds copyright © 1981

Listening to initial sounds.
Associating sounds with letters.

name _____

Color the pictures that begin with the sound /t/ as in turtle.

Letter Sounds copyright © 1981   by J. Marzollo and B. Savage

Listening to initial sounds.
Associating sounds with letters.

name _____

Color the pictures that begin with the sound /v/ as in vase.

by J. Marzollo and B. Savage   Letter Sounds copyright© 1981

Listening to initial sounds.
Associating sounds with letters.

name _____

Color the pictures that begin with the sound /w/ as in wagon.

by J. Marzollo and B. Sonn

Letter Sounds copyright © 1981

Listening to initial sounds.
Associating sounds with letters.

name _____

Color the pictures that have the sound /x/ in them, like box.

by J. Marzollo and B. Savage

Letter Sounds copyright© 1981

Listening to letter sounds.
Associating sounds with letters.

name _____

Color the pictures that begin with the sound /y/ as in yarn.

Letter Sounds copyright©1981 by L. Morrell and S. ...

Listening to initial sounds.
Associating sounds with letters.

name _____

Color the pictures that begin with the sound /z/ as in zebra.

Listening to initial sounds.
Associating sounds with letters.

name _____

Color the pictures that begin with the sound /a/ as in apple.

Listening to initial sounds.
Associating sounds with letters.

name _____

Color the pictures that begin with the sound /e/ as in elephant.

by J. Marzollo and B. Savage

Letter Sounds copyright © 1981

Listening to initial sounds.
Associating sounds with letters.

name _____

Color the pictures that begin with the sound /i/ as in ink.

Letter Sounds copyright © 1981   by J. Mariello and R. Savage

Listening to initial sounds.
Associating sounds with letters.

name _____

Color the pictures that begin with the sound /o/ as in octopus.

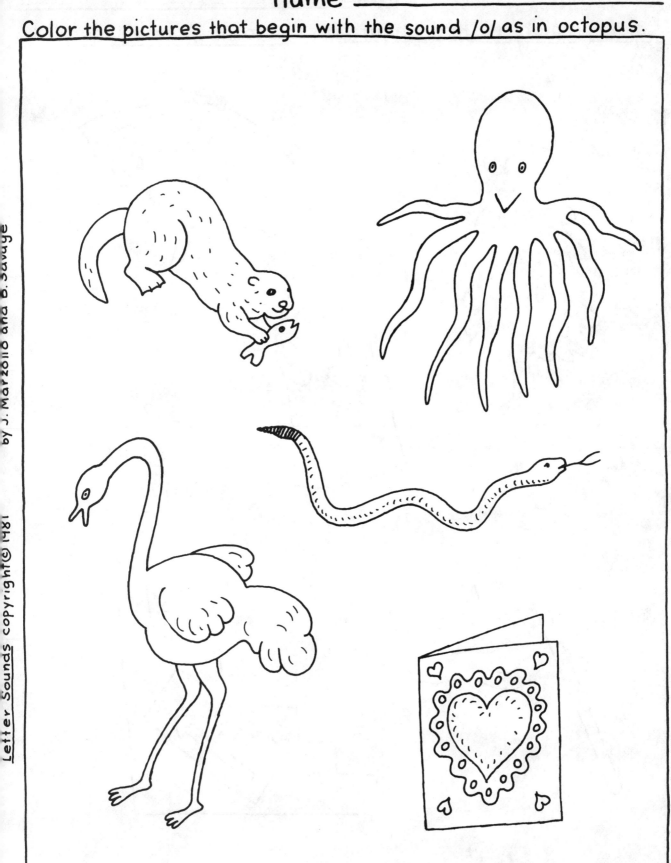

by J. Marzollo and B. Savage

Letter Sounds copyright © 1981

Listening to initial sounds.
Associating sounds with letters.

name _____

Color the pictures that begin with the sound /u/ as in umbrella.

Listening to initial sounds.
Associating sounds with letters.

name _____

Color the pictures that begin with the sound /a/ as in apron.

Letter Sounds copyright © 1981 by S. Marzollo and B. Savage

Listening to initial sounds.
Associating sounds with letters.

name _____

Color the pictures that begin with the sound /e/ as in eagle.

Listening to initial sounds.
Associating sounds with letters.

name _____

Color the pictures that begin with the sound /i/ as in ice cream.

Listening to initial sounds.
Associating sounds with letters.

84

name _____

Color the pictures that begin with the sound /o/ as in oats.

OATS

Listening to initial sounds.
Associating sounds with letters.

by J. Marzollo and B. Savage

Letter Sounds copyright © 1981

name _____

Color the pictures that begin with the sound/u/as in unicycle.

Listening to initial sounds.
Associating sounds with letters.

86

name _____

Color the pictures that begin with the sound /ch/ as in chicken.

Letter Sounds copyright© 1981   by J. Marzollo and R. Cassant

Listening to initial sounds.
Associating sounds with letters.

name _____

Color the pictures that begin with the sound /sh/ as in shoe.

Listening to initial sounds.
Associating sounds with letters.

name _____

Color the pictures that begin with the sound /th/ as in thumb.

Listening to initial sounds.
Associating sounds with letters.

Letter Sounds copyright © 1981   by J. Marzollo and R. Savage

name _____

Draw a line to connect the pictures with rhyming names.

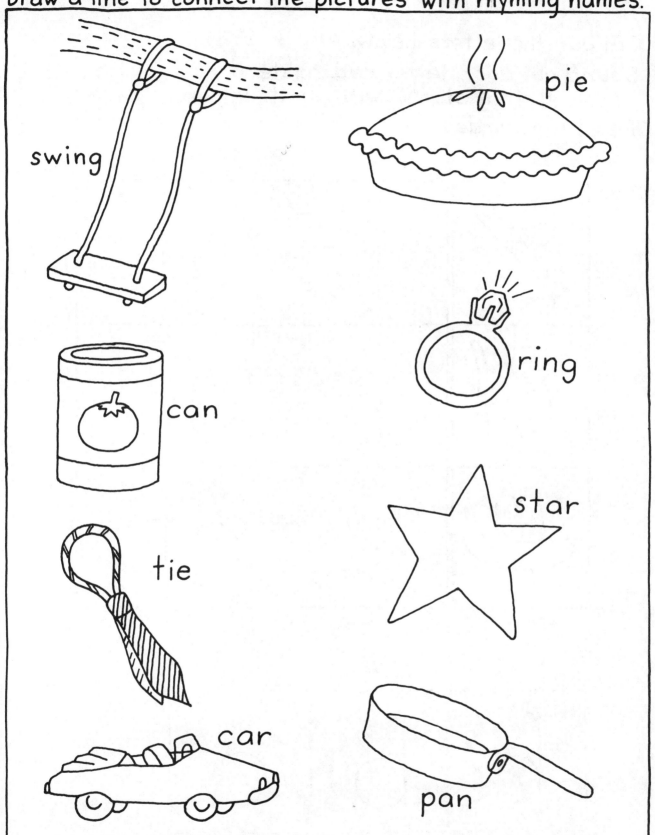

swing

pie

can

ring

tie

star

car

pan

Recognizing words that rhyme.

name _____

Cut out the letters below.
Sound out each letter and paste it next to the
 picture that starts with that letter.
Read the words.

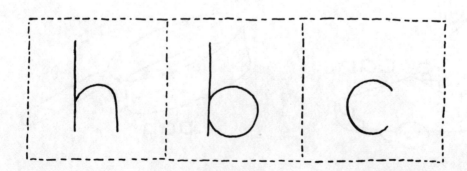

Completing and reading simple word families.

Letter Sounds copyright © 1981   by J. Mardallo and R. Savage

name _____

Cut out the letters below.
Sound out each letter and paste it next to the picture that starts with that letter.
Read the words.

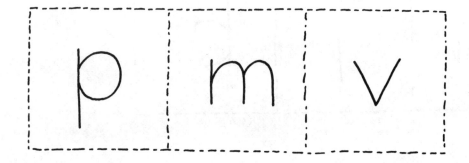

Letter Sounds copyright © 1981 by J. Marzollo and B. Savage

Completing and reading simple word families.

name _____

Cut out the letters below.

Sound out each letter and paste it next to the picture that starts with that letter.

Read the words.

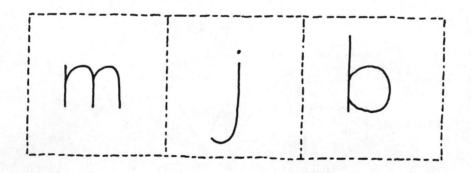

Letter Sounds copyright ©1981   by J. Marzollo and B. Savage

Completing and reading simple word families.

name _____

Cut out the letters below.

Sound out each letter and paste it next to the picture that starts with that letter.

Read the words.

Completing and reading simple word families.

name _____

Cut out the letters and pictures below. Paste the letters before the word endings. Sound out the words. Paste the pictures in the right spaces to go with the words you made.

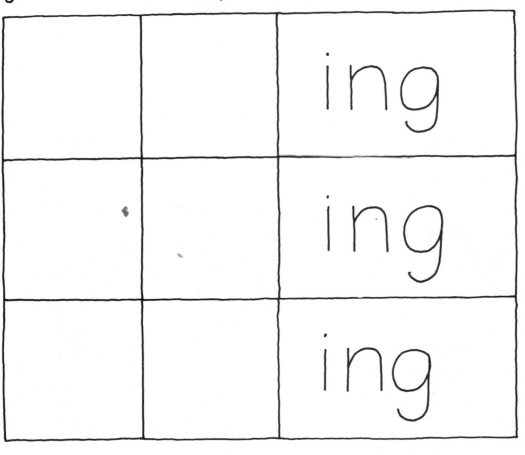

Completing and reading simple word families.

Letter Sounds copyright © 1981   by J. Marzollo and B. Savage

name _____

Cut out the letters and pictures below. Paste the letters before the word endings. Sound out the words. Paste the pictures in the right spaces to go with the words you made.

by J. Marzollo and B. Savage

Letter Sounds copyright © 1981

Completing and reading simple word families.

name _____

Cut out the letters and pictures below. Paste the
letters before the word endings. Sound out the
words. Paste the pictures in the right spaces
to go with the words you made.

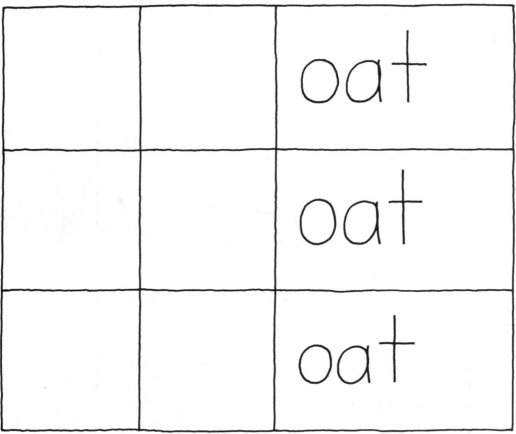

		oat
		oat
		oat

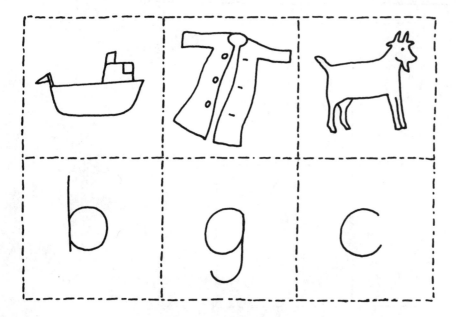

by J. Marzollo and B. Savage

Letter Sounds copyright© 1981

Completing and reading simple word families.

STORYTELLING

Dear Parents,

This year, your child will be bringing home stories and rhymes to share with you. Some of the stories are about simple, everyday events. They will have no text to go with them. Your child will make up a story for the pictures and tell it out loud. Or your child will make up the ending of a story and draw a picture for it.

Some of the stories will be fairy tales. Again, there is no text. Your child will be asked to tell the story out loud. Over the year he or she will build up a collection of six fairy tales to bring home.

We are also studying nursery rhymes. If your child is at the reading stage, we will ask him or her to read the rhymes out loud. If your child is at the prereading stage, we will ask him or her to memorize the rhymes and say them out loud. Nursery rhymes offer children a chance to enjoy rhythm, rhyme, and clever wording.

As your child brings these materials home, please take the time to share them with your child. The overall purpose of the materials is to promote oral language development. So if you let your child entertain you with a story or a rhyme, you'll be helping us teach your child to enjoy speaking out loud.

Thank you,
Your child's teacher

Directions for Teachers

The purpose of this part is to encourage oral language development through the act of storytelling. *Storytelling* provides children with the opportunity to learn how to "read" a page (from left to right and from top to bottom), to make up story endings, to tell stories in the correct order, to act out stories with finger puppets, and to learn nursery rhymes.

The part is divided into three sections: (1) Tell-A-Story, (2) Nursery Rhymes, and (3) Fairy Tales and Finger Puppets. Each section has a special purpose, described below. For each section an instructional model is provided. Feel free to adapt this model in order to use the materials in a way that best suits you and your children.

Section 1: Tell-A-Story   (Pages 105–113)

This section begins with simple stories that are easy to tell and advances to more complex stories for which children are asked to make up their own endings. The first three pages are the simplest; the next three pages are more challenging; and the last three are the most challenging. The purpose of this section is to help children to "read" pictures for information, to make up stories, and to tell out loud the stories they have made up.

Instructional model: Pass out the worksheets. Ask the children to look at the pictures and to think about what is happening in each one. Remind them to look at the pictures in the correct order, following the numbers on the pictures. Ask the children to color the pictures, thinking, as they color, about the story. Assure the children that there is no one correct way to tell the story, as long as it follows the sequence of the pictures. Tell them that you hope that every child in the room will think of a slightly different story.

While the children color, ask them to think of names for the people in the stories. Have them think about what might have happened before the events in the first picture and what might happen if the story continued. Ask the children to keep their ideas secret.

Later, when the pictures have been colored, ask, either in a large or small group setting, for children to volunteer to tell out loud the story that they made up. Compare stories, noting interesting words and names that everyone might like to learn. Encourage each child to take the story home and to tell it out loud there.

The children are asked to draw their own ending for the last three worksheets in this section. If any children protest they can't draw a certain thing, tell them to go ahead and try anyway. Assure them that as long as the drawing is about the story, it will be fine. It is more important for the children to use their imaginations in this exercise than for them to draw realistic pictures.

If you like, have the children cut apart the pictures so that you can staple them into a little book.

Section 2: Nursery Rhymes   (Pages 114–122)

The pages within this section are in no special order. Use them as you like, when you like. The purpose of this section is to help children to listen to rhyme and rhythm, to memorize nursery rhymes, and to enjoy saying nursery rhymes out loud.[1]

Instructional model: Pass out the worksheets. Ask the children if they know the nursery rhyme that goes with the pictures. Some of the children may already know it and be able to say it out loud. If a child stumbles on or forgets certain passages, another child may be able to help him or her out. Encourage those who read to figure out every word of the rhyme by reading it.

Have fun with the rhyme. Don't just read it once. Read it several times dramatically. Ask for children to volunteer to say it out loud for others to hear. Talk about the stories. What actually happened?

Ask the children to color their nursery rhyme worksheets. Tell them that they will make a collection of the nursery rhymes to take home to share. The nursery rhymes can be cut apart and made into little separate books, or you can staple all eight large sheets together with a top cover to make a large take-home book of nursery rhymes.

Section 3: Fairy Tales and Finger Puppets   (Pages 123–148)

The stories within this section are in no special order. Use them as you like. You may wish to spread them over the year or to use them all during a unit on fairy tales and storytelling. The purpose of this section is to help children to learn to tell well-known fairy tales out loud and to encourage them to act out stories through dramatic play.

104

Instructional model: Pass out worksheets for one story. Ask the children to look over all of the pictures. Remind them to "read" the pictures in the correct order.

Ask the children to think about how they would tell the story out loud. Some of the children may know the story, and some may not. Assure them that they can tell it the way they like, as long as what they say goes with the pictures. If many of the children do not know the story, you may wish to have a discussion of what they think the story is about and then follow it up the next day with a special reading of the story from a picture book.

If many of the children are familiar with the story, ask someone to volunteer to tell it out loud. After all of the children learn the story, divide the class into groups of three. Have each group take a turn telling the story. One child tells what is happening on the first page, the next child tells what is happening on the second page, and the third tells what is happening on the last page. Some of the children may enjoy acting the story out for the rest of the class. If so, encourage them to make props and costumes for a show.

Explain to the children that there are different ways to tell the stories. For example, in some versions of *The Three Little Pigs* the wolf ends up being cooked in the pot. In other stories he escapes out the front door. In some stories he eats the first two pigs. In other stories he catches none of them. Tell the children not to be disturbed if the pictures in these stories follow a different story line from the one they already know. Encourage them to bring in books from home or the library with other versions so that you can read these out loud to the class.

The fairy tales can be cut up and stapled into small 12-page books; or the worksheets can be stapled to make large 3-page books. Encourage the children to color their worksheets neatly so that they can save the books and share them with others at home.

After the children are able to tell a story out loud, give them the finger puppets as a reward. Show the children how to make the puppets. First have them color the puppets. Next have the children cut them out carefully. Then have them tape or staple the backs together to form the puppets.

At the end of this section are worksheets for making up, drawing, and telling one's own story. Also included are blank finger puppets, which can be used for the made-up stories or for adding characters to some of the fairy tales. These worksheets will help children to exercise their imaginations and to use their storytelling abilities.

name _____

Color. Make up a story to go with these pictures. Tell it out loud.

by J. Marzollo and B. Savage

Storytelling copyright © 1981

Learning to read a page from left to right and top to bottom.
Learning to make up a story and tell it out loud.

name _____

Color. Make up a story to go with these pictures. Tell it out loud.

1

2

3

4

by J. Marzollo and B. Savage

Storytelling copyright © 1981

Learning to read a page from left to right and top to bottom.
Learning to make up a story and tell it out loud.

name _____

Color. Make up a story to go with these pictures. Tell it out loud.

by J. Marzollo and B. Savage

Storytelling copyright © 1981

Learning to read a page from left to right and top to bottom.
Learning to make up a story and tell it out loud.

name _____

Color. Make up a story to go with these pictures. Tell it out loud.

Learning to read a page from left to right and top to bottom.
Learning to make up a story and tell it out loud.

name _____

Color. Make up a story to go with these pictures. Tell it out loud.

1

2

3

4

by J. Marzollo and B. Savage

Storytelling copyright ©1981

Learning to read a page from left to right and top to bottom.
Learning to make up a story and tell it out loud.

name _____

Color. Make up a story to go with these pictures. Tell it out loud.

1

2

3

4

Learning to read a page from left to right and top to bottom.
Learning to make up a story and tell it out loud.

name _____

Tell a story about these pictures. Draw your own ending.

Learning to read a page from left to right and top to bottom.
Learning to make up a story and tell it out loud.

112

name _____

Tell a story about these pictures. Draw your own ending.

1	2
3	4

Learning to read a page from left to right and top to bottom.
Learning to make up a story and tell it out loud.

name _____

Tell a story about these pictures. Draw your own ending.

1	2
3	4

Learning to read a page from left to right and top to bottom.
Learning to make up a story and tell it out loud.

name _____

Color. Learn the nursery rhyme. Tell it out loud.

1

Hickory Dickory Dock,

2

The mouse ran up the clock;

3

The clock struck one,

4
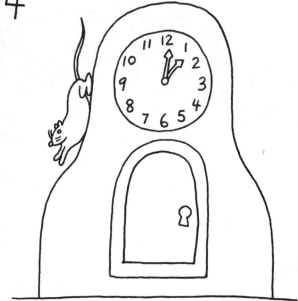

The mouse ran down, Hickory Dickory Dock.

Learning to read a page from left to right and top to bottom.
Learning to tell nursery rhymes.

name _____

Color. Learn the nursery rhyme. Tell it out loud.

1	2
Humpty Dumpty sat on a wall,	Humpty Dumpty had a great fall;
3	4
All the king's horses and all the king's men	Couldn't put Humpty Dumpty together again.

Learning to read a page from left to right and top to bottom.
Learning to tell nursery rhymes.

name _____

Color. Learn the nursery rhyme. Tell it out loud.

1

Jack and Jill
went up a hill

2

To fetch a pail
of water;

3

Jack fell down and
broke his crown,

4

And Jill came
tumbling after.

Learning to read a page from left to right and top to bottom.
Learning to tell nursery rhymes.

name _____

Color. Learn the nursery rhyme. Tell it out loud.

1

Pat-a-cake, pat-a-cake baker's man,

2

Make me a cake as fast as you can;

3

Pat it and stretch it and mark it with a B,

4

And put it in the oven for Baby and me.

Learning to read a page from left to right and top to bottom.
Learning to tell nursery rhymes.

name _____

Color. Learn the nursery rhyme. Tell it out loud.

1

Little Bo-Peep has lost her sheep,

2

And can't tell where to find them;

3

Leave them alone, and they'll come home

4

And bring their tails behind them.

by J. Marzollo and B. Savage   Storytelling copyright © 1981

Learning to read a page from left to right and top to bottom.
Learning to tell nursery rhymes.

name _____

Color. Learn the nursery rhyme. Tell it out loud.

by J. Marzollo and B. Savage

Storytelling copyright ©1981

1

Baa, baa, black sheep,
have you any wool?
Yes sir, yes sir,
three bags full;

2

One for my master,

3

One for my dame,

4

And one for the little boy
who lives down the lane.

Learning to read a page from left to right and top to bottom.
Learning to tell nursery rhymes.

name _____

Color. Learn the nursery rhyme. Tell it out loud.

Once I saw a little bird
come hop, hop, hop,

So I cried, "Little bird,
will you stop, stop, stop?"

I was going to the window
to say, "How do you do?"

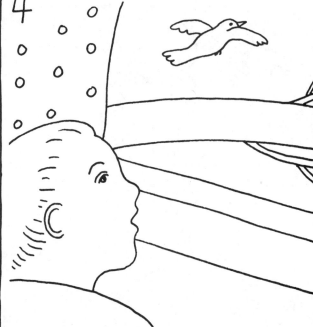

But he shook his little tail
and far away he flew.

Learning to read a page from left to right and top to bottom.
Learning to tell nursery rhymes.

name _____

Color. Learn the nursery rhyme. Tell it out loud.

by J. Marzollo and B. Savage

Storytelling copyright © 1981

1

Mary, Mary,
quite contrary,

2

How does your
garden grow?

3

With cockle shells
and silver bells

4

And cowslips all
in a row.

Learning to read a page from left to right and top to bottom.
Learning to tell nursery rhymes.

name _____

Color. Learn the nursery rhyme. Tell it out loud.

1

Hey, diddle, diddle, the cat and the fiddle,

2

The cow jumped over the moon;

3

The little dog laughed to see such sport,

4

And the dish ran away with the spoon.

by J. Marzollo and B. Savage

Storytelling copyright ©1981

Learning to read a page from left to right and top to bottom
Learning to tell nursery rhymes

123

Color. Tell the story out loud.

1

Goldilocks and the Three Bears

name _____

by J. Marzollo and B. Savage

Storytelling copyright©1981

2

3

4

Oral language development. Story sequencing.
Reading pictures from left to right and top to bottom.

by J. Marzollo and B. Savage

Storytelling copyright © 1981

by J. Marzollo and D. Savage

Storytelling copyright ©1981

Color. Cut on dotted lines.
Tape or staple in back to form puppets.

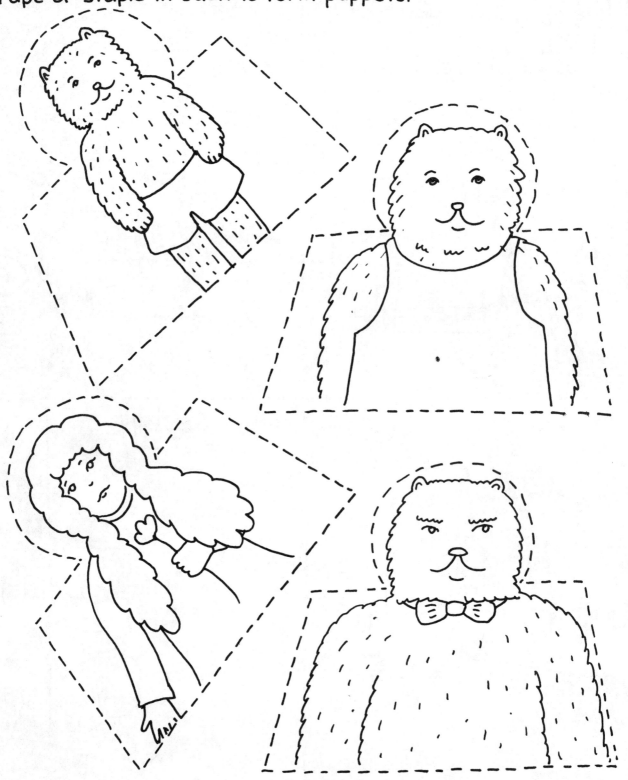

Oral language development.

Color. Tell the story out loud.

by J. Marzollo and B. Savage

Storytelling copyright © 1981

1 The Three Little Pigs

name _____

2

3

4

Oral language development. Story sequencing.
Reading pictures from left to right and top to bottom.

by J. Marzollo and B. Savage · Storytelling copyright © 1981

by J. Marzollo and B. Savage

Storytelling copyright ©1981

Color. Cut on dotted lines.
Tape or staple in back to form puppets.

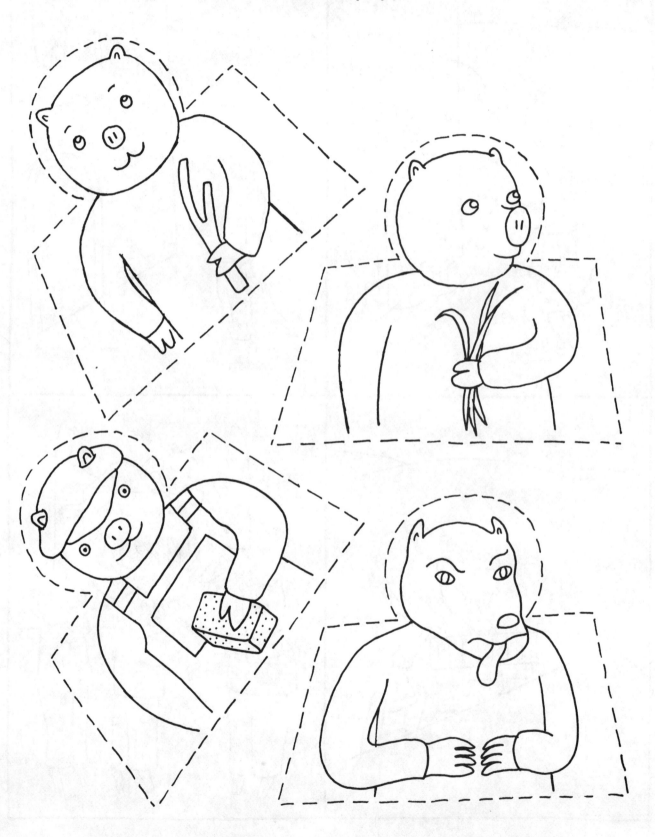

by J. Marzollo and R. Savage

Storytelling copyright © 1981

Oral language development.

Color. Tell the story out loud.

by J. Marzollo and B. Savage

Storytelling copyright © 1981

1
Jack and the Beanstalk

name _____

2

3

4

Oral language development. Story sequencing.
Reading pictures from left to right and top to bottom.

Storytelling copyright©1981 by J. Marzollo and R. Savage

by J. Marzollo and B. Savage

Storytelling copyright©1981

Color. Cut on dotted lines.
Tape or staple in back to form puppets.

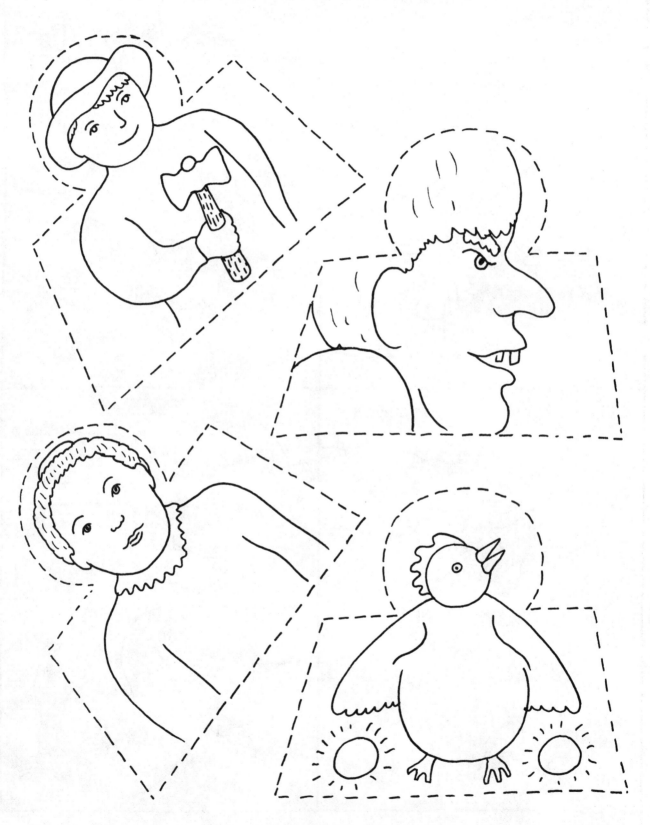

Oral language development.

by J. Marzollo and B. Savage

Storytelling copyright © 1981

Color. Tell the story out loud.

1

Cinderella

name _____

by J. Marzollo and B. Savage

Storytelling copyright©1981

2

3

4

Oral language development. Story sequencing.
Reading pictures from left to right and top to bottom.

by J. Marzollo and B. Savage

Storytelling copyright © 1981

by J. Marzollo and B. Savage

Storytelling copyright ©1981

Color. Cut on dotted lines.
Tape or staple in back to form puppets.

Oral language development.

by J. Marzollo and B. Savage

Storytelling copyright ©1981

Color. Cut on dotted lines.
Tape or staple in back to form puppets.

by J. Marzollo and B. Savage

Storytelling copyright© 1981

Oral language development.

by J. Marzollo and B. Savage

Storytelling copyright © 1981

1
A Story about Me

name _____

2
This is what I look like.

3

My favorite toy is _____.

4

My favorite animal is _____.

144

<table>
<tr>
<td>5

My teacher is
_____.</td>
<td>6

My favorite color
is _____.</td>
</tr>
<tr>
<td>7

My favorite book
is_____.</td>
<td>8

Something I don't
like is _____.</td>
</tr>
</table>

Storytelling copyright ©1981 by J. Marzollo and B. Sawyer

9

A person I love is
_____.

10

Here's a picture
of my house.

11

Here's a picture of
my favorite food.

12

Here's what I look
like when I go
to sleep.
          The End.

Draw and color. Cut on dotted lines.
Tape or staple in back to form puppets.

by J. Marzollo and B. Savage

Storytelling copyright © 1981

Oral language development.

1

name_____

2

3

4

by J. Arizona and D. Savage

copyright ©1181

Storytelling copyright © 1981 by J. Marzollo and B. Savage

THINKING SKILLS

Dear Parents,

This year your child will be bringing home worksheets that give practice in observing details and logical thinking. Sometimes the worksheets will be homework. In these cases, your child is to do the work and bring it back to school the next day. Sometimes your child will have completed the worksheet in school and will be bringing it home to show you what he or she has done.

Some of the worksheets will show your child's skill in visual discrimination, that is, the ability to look at a picture, letter, or word and see that it is different from other pictures, letters, or words. Often your child will be asked to find something that is the same as (or different from) other things on the page. After learning to distinguish things that are similar or different, your child will move on to worksheets dealing with the more advanced skills of sorting and classifying.

On some of the worksheets, the pictures are out of order. Your child will put these pictures in logical order and tell a story about them. Many of the skills covered in this series of worksheets are related to reading skills.

Please go over these worksheets with your child. Ask your child to explain what he or she has done. Your child will be pleased with your interest and will be proud to share the work with you.

Thank you,

Your child's teacher

Directions for Teachers

The purpose of this part is to help children observe details and think logically. The part is divided into three sections: (1) Same and Different, (2) Sorting and Classifying, and (3) Sequencing and Logical Storytelling. Visual discrimination skills are emphasized in the first two sections. Many of the skills covered in the part are important prereading skills.

All of the pages can be colored by the children. Often coloring is inherent in the task involved. In every case coloring is a valid activity for strengthening hand muscles and improving eye-hand coordination. For specific page directions, see below.

Section 1:
Same and Different   (Pages 155–175)

Pages 155–157

Ask the children to find the objects that match and to color matching pictures the same. They can color the other objects differently. Depending on the abilities of the children, they can use a single color for an entire object or use a combination of colors.

Pages 158–160

Ask the children to look carefully at the letters or words. Some of the children may be able to read the words on pages 159 and 160. The words on page 159 provide an opportunity to discuss the concept of opposites.

Pages 161–163

In these exercises, the children find the object that is different and change it to be the same as the others. On page 161 the objects are faces; on page 162 the objects are letters; on page 163 the objects are numbers.

Pages 164–173

These pages are to be used in pairs. The first page in each pair contains matching cards, which are to be colored and cut out by the children. The second page in the pair is the matching board. Have the children color it to match the cards. Then they can play a Lotto-like matching game, matching the cards to the pictures on the matching board. Do not rush the preparation of each game. On the first day, have the children color the cards. On the second day, the children color the board to match the cards. On the third day, the children cut out the cards and play the matching game. You may want to save certain matching games for special units of study. Pages 164–165 are about birds; pages 166–167 are about T-shirts; pages 168–169 are about books; pages 170–171 are about rhyming words; and pages 172–173 are about things that go together. Encourage the children to take care of their matching games. Show the children how to make storage envelopes out of construction paper and keep the games in these envelopes.

Pages 174–175

On these worksheets, children match mittens and socks. They can also look at the designs on real socks and mittens. On a cold winter day, put everyone's mittens on a table and play a matching game with them. Have the children take a look at their socks. Teach them words for designs (stripes, ribbed, cable-knit, argyle) and new words for colors (lavender, tan). Talk about sorting socks at home after doing laundry.

Section 2:
Sorting and Classifying   (Pages 176–188)

Pages 176–183

Pages 176–177 are used together and are a model for the other pages in this section. Ask the children to color the baseball hats. They should be sure to keep the team colors consistent. Then the children cut out the hat cards. Next, show the children how to sort and "put away" the hats in the "boxes" on page 177.

Page 178 provides an all-purpose sorting box to be used for the cards on pages 179–183. Categories are not specified for these pages. The children must look at the cards and decide for themselves how to classify them. You may want to save certain pages for special units of study: page 179 for a unit on food and nutrition, page 180 for a unit on animals, page 181 for number recognition, page 182 for upper case letter recognition, and page 183 for lower case letter recognition.

Pages 184–185

On these worksheets, the children put an X on the object that is not like the others. Ask them to color the other objects if you like. Pages 184–185 are the easiest to do.

Pages 186–188

Have the children circle the things that do not belong. You can also ask them to color the things that go together, if you wish. Before the children work on page 186, discuss the difference between numbers and letters.

Section 3:
Sequencing and
Logical Storytelling (Pages 189–198)

Pages 189–198

These worksheets are designed to be used in pairs. On the first worksheet in each pair, the pictures are out of order. The children should color them, then cut them out. The second page of the pair contains blank spaces. The children are asked to place the pictures in order from left to right and top to bottom to tell a logical story. Check the placement of the pictures. If the story is logical, the child may paste the pictures in place. The child can then tell the story out loud. If a child has placed the pictures out of sequence, ask to hear the child's explanation before you say it's wrong. Children think of ingenious and logical ways to arrange pictures. The important thing is that the child think logically and be able to express his or her thoughts.

name _____

Find the ones that match. Color them the same.

  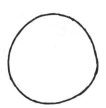 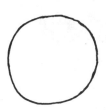

by J. Marzollo and B. Savage

Thinking Skills copyright ©1981

Visual discrimination.

Understanding the concept "same as."

name _____

Find the ones that match. Color them the same.

by J. Marzollo and B. Savage

Thinking Skills copyright ©1981

Visual discrimination.

Understanding the concept "same as."

157

name _____

Find the ones that match. Color them the same.

by J. Marzollo and B. Savage

Thinking Skills copyright©1981

Visual discrimination.

Understanding the concept "same as."

name _____

Circle the one in each group that is different.

k	k	k
k	f	
k	k	k

o	o	o
	o	o
o	p	o

A	A	A
A	A	
V	A	A

z	z	z
	z	z
z	z	y

m	n	m
m	m	
m	m	m

b	d	d
d	d	
d	d	d

Visual discrimination.

Understanding the concept "different."

by J. Marzollo and B. Savage
Thinking Skills copyright© 1981

name _____

Circle the one in each group that is different.

little   big   big
 	
   big   big
 	
big   big   big
	GO GO STOP
	
	   GO GO
	
	GO GO GO

open   open   open
 	
  closed   open
 	
open   open   open
	in in in
	
	  out in
	
	in in in

UP   UP   UP
 	
  UP   DOWN
 	
UP   UP   UP
	EXIT EXIT EXIT
	
	  ENTRANCE EXIT
	
	EXIT EXIT EXIT

by J. Marzollo and B. Savage

Thinking Skills copyright©1981

Visual discrimination.

Understanding the concept "different."

name _____

Circle the one in each group that is different.

red   red
 	
   rod
 	
red   red
	bat bat
	
	   bat
	
	bit bat

pan   pan
 	
   pan
 	
pan   pin
	run run
	
	   ran
	
	run run

dog   dog
 	
   dog
 	
dig   dog
	at at
	
	   ate
	
	at at

Visual discrimination.

Understanding the concept "different."

by J. Marzollo and B. Savage   Thinking Skills copyright © 1981

name _____

Find the one that's different. Make it like the others.

by J. Marzollo and B. Savage

Thinking skills copyright © 1981

Visual discrimination.

Understanding the concept "different."

name _____

Find the one that's different. Make it like the others.

A A A A A A

H H H H -H -H

N N N N N N

L L L L I L

C E E E E E

by J. Marzollo and B. Savage

Thinking Skills copyright ©1981

Visual discrimination.

Understanding the concept "different."

name _____

Find the one that's different. Make it like the others.

2	2	2	2	2
4	4	L	4	4
5	5	5	5	5
7	7	7	7	⌐
9	9	○	9	9

by J. Marzollo and B. Savage

Thinking Skills copyright ©1981

Visual discrimination.
Understanding the concept "different."

name _____

Bird Matching Cards. Cut on the dotted lines.

by J. Marzollo and B. Savage

Thinking Skills copyright © 1981

These cards are to be used with page 165.

name _____

Bird Matching Board. Match the cards here.

by J. Marzollo and B. Savage

Thinking Skills copyright ©1981

Visual discrimination.

Understanding the concept "same as."

name _____

T-Shirt Matching Cards. Cut on the dotted lines.

by J. Marzollo and B. Savage

Thinking Skills copyright©1981

These cards are to be used with page 167.

167

name _____

T-Shirt Matching Board. Match the cards here.

by J. Marzollo and B. Savage

Thinking Skills copyright ©1981

Visual discrimination.
Understanding the concept "same as."

168

Book Matching Cards. Cut on the dotted lines.

YOU

STARS

Water

STOP and GO

IN and OUT

DOGS

Dolls

ME

Zebras

by J. Marzollo and B. Savage

Thinking Skills copyright©1981

These cards are to be used with page 169.

name _____

Book Matching Board. Match the cards here.

by J. Marzollo and B. Savage

Thinking Skills copyright©1981

IN and OUT

STARS

Zebras

ME

YOU

Dolls

STOP and GO

DOGS

Water

Visual discrimination.
Understanding the concept "same as."

name _____

Rhyming Matching Cards. Cut on the dotted lines.

by J. Marzollo and B. Savage

Thinking Skills copyright ©1981

These cards are to be used with page 171.

name _____

Rhyming Matching Board. Match the cards here.

by J. Marzollo and B. Savage

Thinking Skills copyright©1981

Visual discrimination.
Auditory discrimination.

name _____

Go-Together Matching Cards. Cut on the dotted lines.

by J. Marzollo and B. Savage

Thinking Skills copyright © 1981

These cards are to be used with page 173.

name _____

Go-Together Matching Board. Match the cards here.

by J. Marzollo and B. Savage

Thinking Skills copyright©1981

Visual discrimination.
Understanding the concept "goes together."

name _____

Draw lines to connect the mittens that go together.

by J. Marzollo and B. Savage

Thinking Skills copyright© 1981

Visual discrimination.

Understanding the concept "same as."

name _____

Find the one that is not like the others. Put an X on it.

by J. Marzollo and B. Savage

Thinking Skills copyright©1981

Visual discrimination.
Sorting and classifying.

name _____

Draw lines to connect the socks that go together.

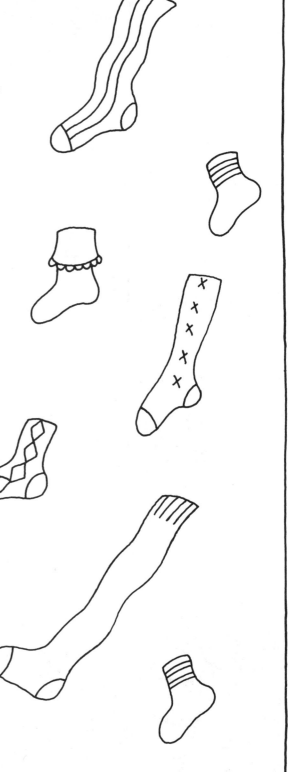

by J. Marzollo and B. Savage

Thinking Skills copyright © 1981

Visual discrimination.

Understanding the concept "same as."

name _____

Baseball Cap Sorting Cards. Cut on the dotted lines.

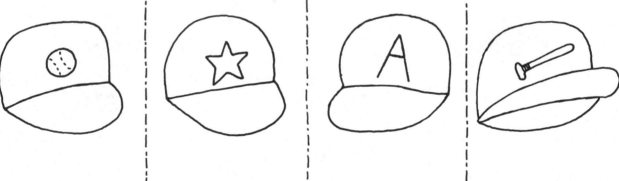

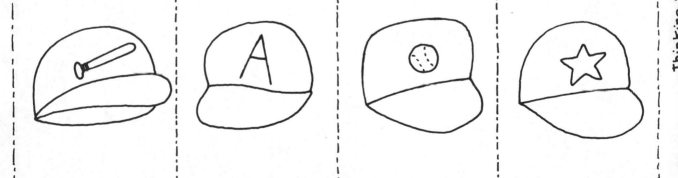

by J. Marzollo and B. Savage

Thinking Skills copyright © 1981

These cards are to be used with page 177.

name _____

Baseball Cap Sorting Boxes. Sort the cards here.

by J. Marzollo and B. Savage

Thinking Skills copyright©1981

Visual discrimination.
Sorting and classifying.

name _____

Sorting Boxes. Sort cards here.

by J. Marzollo and B. Savage

Thinking Skills copyright©1981

Visual discrimination.
Sorting and classifying.

name _____

Fruit Sorting Cards. Cut on the dotted lines.

by J. Marzollo and B. Savage

Thinking Skills copyright©1981

These cards are to be used with page 178.

name _____

Animal Sorting Cards. Cut on dotted lines.

by J. Marzollo and B. Savage

Thinking Skills copyright © 1981

These cards are to be used with page 178.

name _____

Number Sorting Cards. Cut on the dotted lines.

2	3	4	5
3	2	3	5
4	5	2	4
5	2	3	4

by J. Marzollo and B. Savage

Thinking Skills copyright © 1981

These cards are to be used with page 178.

182

name _____

Letter Sorting Cards. Cut on the dotted lines.

A	X	V	W
V	W	X	A
X	A	V	W
A	W	V	X

by J. Marzollo and B. Savage

Thinking Skills copyright ©1981

These cards are to be used with page 178.

name _____

Letter Sorting Cards. Cut on the dotted lines.

b	d	a	d
a	p	b	d
d	b	p	a
p	a	p	b

by J. Marzollo and B. Savage

Thinking Skills copyright © 1981

These cards are to be used with page 178.

name _____

Find the one that is not like the others. Put an X on it.

by J. Marzollo and B. Savage

Thinking Skills copyright©1981

Visual discrimination.
Sorting and classifying.

name _____

Circle the thing that doesn't belong.

A F 2 G

4 H 3 6

e f 7 c

9 5 g 3

y 9 6 2

by J. Marzollo and B. Savage

Thinking Skills copyright © 1981

Visual discrimination.
Sorting and classifying.

name _____

Circle the thing that doesn't belong.

Visual discrimination.

Classification.

name _____

Circle the thing that doesn't belong.

by J. Marzollo and B. Savage

Thinking Skills copyright © 1981

Visual discrimination.
Classification.

name _____

Cat Pictures. Cut on the dotted lines.

by J. Marzollo and B. Savage

Thinking Skills copyright©1981

These pictures are to be used with page 190.

name _____

Cat Story. Paste the pictures in order. Tell the story.

by J. Marzollo and B. Savage

Thinking Skills copyright© 1981

Sequencing.
Logical storytelling.

name _____

Water Pictures. Cut on the dotted lines.

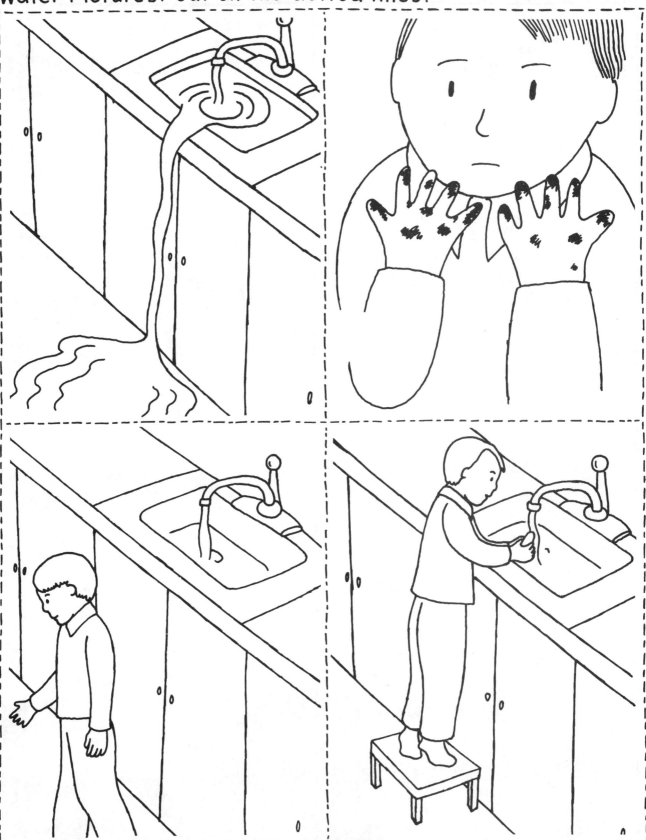

by J. Marzollo and B. Savage

Thinking Skills copyright©1981

These pictures are to be used with page 192.

name _____

Water Story. Paste the pictures in order. Tell the story.

by J. Marzollo and B. Savage

Thinking Skills copyright © 1981

Sequencing.
Logical storytelling.

name _____

Cake Pictures. Cut on the dotted lines.

by J. Marzollo and B. Savage

Thinking Skills copyright © 1981

These pictures are to be used with page 194.

name _____

Cake Story. Paste the pictures in order. Tell the story.

by J. Marzollo and B. Savage

Thinking Skills copyright©1981

194

Sequencing.
Logical storytelling.

name _____

<u>Snowman</u> <u>Pictures</u>. Cut <u>on</u> the <u>dotted</u> lines.

by J. Marzollo and B. Savage

<u>Thinking</u> <u>Skills</u> copyright©1981

These pictures are to be used with page 196.

196

name _____

Snowman Story. Paste the pictures in order. Tell the story.

by J. Marzollo and B. Savage

Thinking Skills copyright© 1981

Sequencing.
Logical storytelling.

name _____

Boat Pictures. Cut on the dotted lines.

by J. Marzollo and B. Savage

Thinking Skills copyright©1981

These pictures are to be used with page 198.

name _____

Boat Story. Paste the pictures in order. Tell the story.

Sequencing.
Logical storytelling.

by J. Marzollo and B. Savage

Thinking Skills copyright©1981

ABOUT THE AUTHORS

Jean Marzollo is a free-lance writer and editor whose books include *Learning Through Play, Supertot,* and *Superkids,* all published by Harper & Row. She is also the author of many books for children, including the critically acclaimed *Close Your Eyes* (Dial). Her collaborator, Beth Savage, is a free-lance artist. Both authors live in Cold Spring, New York.

CHARLES BENNETT
1271 GROVELAND LANE
LAKELAND,FL 33811